THANET'S TRAMWAYS

Robert J Harley

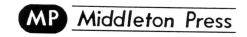 Middleton Press

Cover picture details can be seen in caption 15. The cover colours are similar to those used on the trams in their final years.

First published February 1993

ISBN 1 873793 11 1

© *Middleton Press 1993*

Design - Deborah Goodridge

Published by Middleton Press
        Easebourne Lane
        Midhurst
        West Sussex
        GU29 9AZ
        Tel: (0730) 813169

Printed & bound by Biddles Ltd,
        Guildford and Kings Lynn

Model Railway Workshop

Prop: JOHN BELL

Retail Unit 34,
Stapehill Abbey & Gardens,
276 Wimborne Road West,
Wimborne,
Dorset, BH21 2EB.

Preferred Delivery
& Postal Address
7 Juniper Close,
Ferndown,
Dorset, BH22 9UB.
01202 - 891521
24 Hour Answerphone

With Compliments

INTRODUCTION AND ACKNOWLEDGEMENTS

The Isle of Thanet tramway system connected the towns of Margate, Broadstairs and Ramsgate on the Kent coast. Throughout the research for this book it was obvious that there was a great deal of affection for the trams and that the world had become duller by their passing. I should therefore like to dedicate this work to the small, but versatile staff at St. Peter's depot who kept the wheels turning and to all ex-employees of the company who provided the area with reliable and efficient public transport.

I must thank D.W.K.Jones for his very valuable assistance in supplying photographs, information and personal reminiscences. George Gundry invited me to his home and regaled me with a fund of stories and memories; he has remarkable powers of recall dating from his first photographic trip to Ramsgate in 1922. Rosemary Thacker, the librarian at the National Tramway Museum, and Penny Ward, the heritage officer for Thanet libraries, were both very helpful in locating useful information. John Nightingale has conducted local research for me and his efforts are much appreciated. Brian and Rene Burnell who are old family friends, first introduced me to the area and I thank them both for recent hospitality on my return visit.

The following individuals have assisted in the project, and I thank them all: B.Boddy, C.Carter, D.G.Collyer, W.J.Haynes, J.Hiscott, C.M.Jackson, H.J.Patterson Rutherford, E.Shields and L.T.Woodruff.

My wife and children have been very supportive, putting up with detours from the beach at Westgate to sites of tramway interest. I can only say they have been very tolerant!

CONTENTS

1	Westbrook
8	Margate
24	Cliftonville
41	Kentish woods and fields
51	St. Peter's
59	Broadstairs Top Road
65	Broadstairs Main Line
	Ramsgate -
71	Belle Vue Road
74	Wellington Crescent
76	Madeira Walk
87	Ramsgate Harbour
93	Station Terminus
98	Rolling Stock
110	Trouble at Westbrook
112	Overhead
116	Trackwork
120	Staff

GEOGRAPHICAL SETTING

The Isle of Thanet as its name suggests was once entirely separate from the English mainland, but over centuries the actions of wind, weather and tides have eroded this isolation. Thanet now forms a promontory of the county of Kent at the confluence of the English Channel and the North Sea. Chalk cliffs rise steeply along many parts of the coast and some of the roads subsequently used by the tramways contain appreciable gradients. The soil is very fertile and cornfields were once a common sight on the journey between the three main towns.

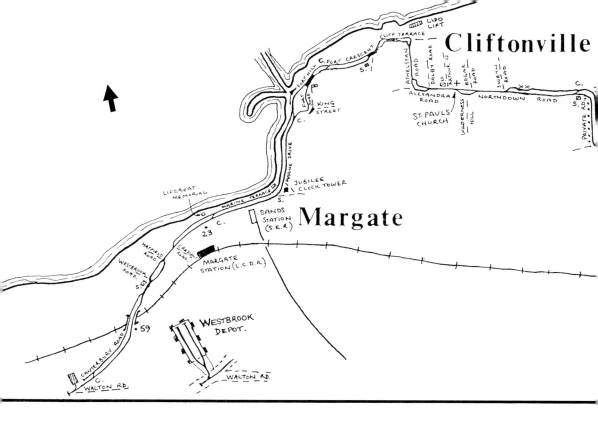

HISTORICAL BACKGROUND

The Romans came to Thanet establishing forts at Reculver and Richborough, subsequently they were followed by waves of invading Saxons and Vikings. The landing of St. Augustine in 597 and the conversion of the Kentish King Ethelbert in the neighbouring city of Canterbury makes this area the cradle of Christianity in England. Another invasion occurred with the arrival of the railways in 1847, bringing an influx of trippers from London to Margate and Ramsgate. Broadstairs retained a fishing village atmosphere and its most famous nineteenth century resident was the author Charles Dickens, who wrote much of "David Copperfield" whilst staying at Bleak House. A short lived horse tramway connected St. Peters with Broadstairs; a mile of track was laid for a solitary horse car, the project then failed, the track was ripped up in 1884 and the tram sold to South Shields,

eventually being resold to Douglas, Isle of Man, where incredibly it still survives. The electric tramway was promoted by William Martin Murphy, later chairman of the Dublin United Tramways, and a well known entrepreneur and visionary in the electric traction field. The line was built under the auspices of the Light Railways Act; construction started in 1899 and the route opened throughout from Westbrook to Ramsgate on 6th July 1901. The name of the undertaking was the "Isle of Thanet Electric Tramways and Lighting Company." It was an instant success serving a natural traffic route. After an initial crop of accidents and teething troubles with the new bogie cars, the tramway settled down to a profitable existence.

In 1913 the first motor buses were put into service basically as feeders for the trams; at this time a record number of people were being

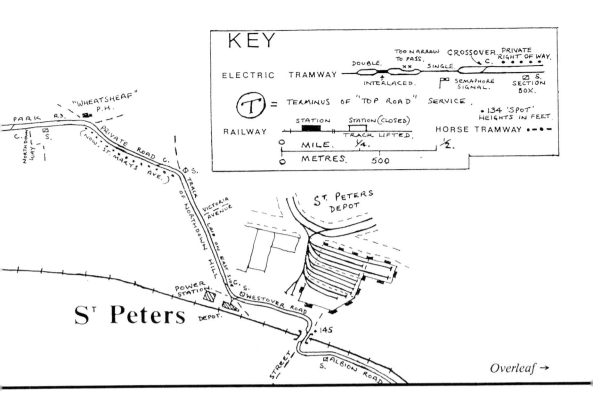

Overleaf →

transported and on warm summer days the eleven miles of route saw the whole fleet of sixty cars in operation crewed by every available employee, including depot fitters, overhead linesmen and permanent way staff. World War I started in August 1914 and had an immediate effect on passenger and fleet maintenance levels, so that by November 1918 the cars and track were in poor condition. The company set about putting matters in order and during the post war years instituted a programme of car rebuilding which continued until just before abandonment. The track was repaired and many roads were repaved as new housing appeared along the route. A change of name in 1924 to the "Isle of Thanet Electric Supply Company" reflected the growing dominance of the domestic supply sector and from then on the tramway side was the lesser partner. However, the service on the "main

line" still needed a car every few minutes at peak times and the journey remained a favourite for thousands of holiday makers. In spite of the popularity of the tramway the storm clouds were gathering and in 1935 the councils of Margate, Ramsgate and Broadstairs requested the undertaking to consider abandonment. In October 1936 operation of the company's bus services passed to the East Kent Roadcar Company and at the end of the year the nearby Dover Corporation Tramways also fell victim to East Kent. The writing was on the wall and the trams continued for a few months until Wednesday 24th March 1937 when car 20 closed the system.

Thus the Isle of Thanet tramways passed away. The sight and sound of a fully loaded tramcar swaying across the tree lined cornfields, the motors humming and the trolley swishing on the wire, faded for ever.

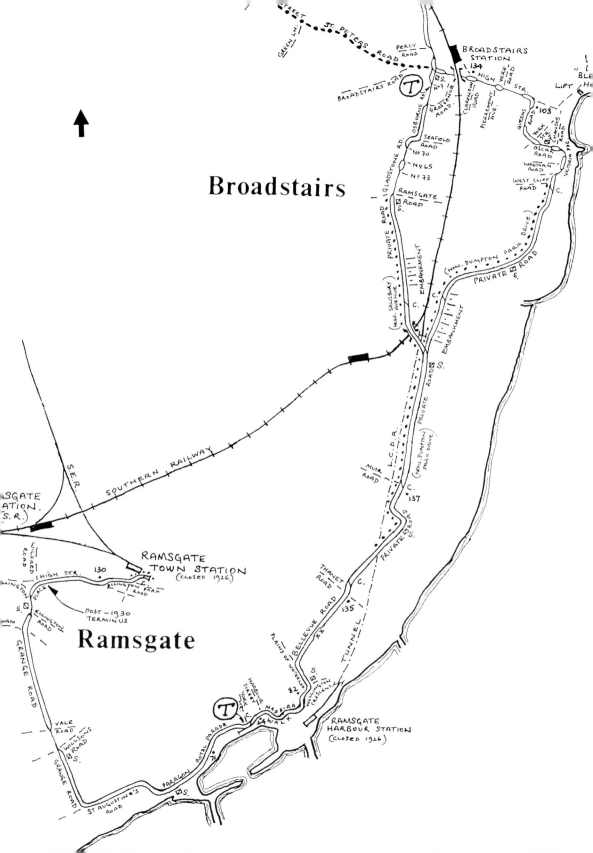

WESTBROOK

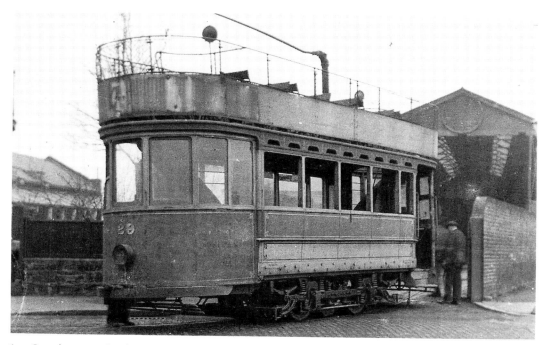

1. Our journey begins at Westbrook depot reached by a single track spur from the terminus. Car 29 looking rather worse for wear has halted at the entrance whilst a crew member switches the points. During the 1920s many similar trams were taken out of service to await renovation as time and materials permitted. (D.W.K.Jones)

2. In 1992 three enthusiasts of a new generation, Matthew, Abigail and Rachel Harley, stand outside the depot which was still substantially intact. (R.J.Harley)

3. The old depot building is now (1992) owned by the Electricity Board. The 3ft. 6ins. gauge tracks still lead to the stabling shed which remarkably has survived in this age of wholesale urban redevelopment. (R.J.Harley)

→

5. Outside the depot gates in Canterbury Road the driver takes a couple of minutes break whilst the conductor swings the trolley for the return journey. Behind car 59 is the shortest bracket arm standard on the system which also carries the "All Cars Stop Here" sign. There is evidence of impending road widening with new kerb stones stacked to the right of the tram. (C.Carter)

4. A tram lays over in the 1922 summer sunshine. The gates of the depot can be glimpsed through the lower saloon windows. These windows were an odd four and a half bay configuration indicating that this car is from the 21-40 series whose original bodies were shortened and placed on four wheel trucks. (G.L.Gundry)

6. Road works continue as car 5 prepares to depart. In the distance is the tower of All Saints Church; another tram waits to use the single track terminal. (D.W.K.Jones)

7. A late afternoon in summer and time for a chat outside the Nayland Rock Hotel. There is an air of relaxed gentility as car 12 with the highway to itself ambles towards Margate front. The centre poles on this stretch were removed in 1907. (G.L.Gundry Coll.)

MARGATE

8. "Friend to All Nations." The Lifeboat Memorial on Marine Terrace serves as a reminder of the heroic and selfless devotion shown by Margate crews over the decades. In calm summer weather car 4 loads seaside trippers whilst a marvellous collection of baby carriages is wheeled along the promenade. (R.J.Harley Coll.)

ONE PENNY.

TO	FROM
S. E. Station, Ramsgate,	York Street, Ramsgate.
Pegwell Road,	Plains of Waterloo.
York Street, Ramsgate,	Thanet Road.
Thanet Road,	Broadstairs Front.
Broadstairs Front	Broadstairs Station.
Broadstairs Station,	Tramway Dépôt.
Tramway Dépôt,	Northdown Corner.
Wheatsheaf,	Athelstan Road.
Northdown Corner,	King St., Margate Harbour.
Athelstan Road, Cliftonville end.	Margate Station.
King St., Margate Harbour,	Westbrook, Margate.

THREE HALF PENCE.

Thanet Road,	Broadstairs Station.

TWOPENCE.

S. E. Station, Ramsgate,	Thanet Road.
York Street, Ramsgate,	Broadstairs Station.
Thanet Road,	Tramway Dépôt.
Broadstairs Station,	Northdown Corner.
Tramway Dépôt,	King St., Margate Harbour.
Wheatsheaf,	Margate Station.
Northdown Corner,	Westbrook, Margate.

THREEPENCE.

TO	FROM
S. E. Station, Ramsgate,	Broadstairs Station.
York Street, Ramsgate,	Tramway Dépôt.
Thanet Road,	Northdown Corner.
Broadstairs Station,	King Street, Margate Harbour.
Tramway Dépôt,	Westbrook, Margate.

FOURPENCE.

S. E. Station, Ramsgate,	Tramway Dépôt.
York Street, Ramsgate,	Northdown Corner.
Broadstairs Station,	Westbrook, Margate.
Thanet Road,	King Street, Margate Harbour.

FIVEPENCE.

S. E. Station, Ramsgate,	Northdown Corner.
York Street, Ramsgate,	King Street, Margate Harbour.
Thanet Road,	Westbrook.

SIXPENCE.

S. E. Station, Ramsgate,	Westbrook, Margate.

EIGHTPENCE RETURN.

York St., Ramsgate,	King St., Margate Harbour.

TENPENCE RETURN.

S. E. Station, Ramsgate,	Westbrook, Margate.

9. The beach is filled with holiday makers in this turn of the century scene. In the middle of the picture car 51 has just cleared the much used short working crossover outside the forecourt of Margate Sands station visible on the right and featured in *"Dover to Ramsgate"* - Middleton Press. (R.J.Harley Coll.)

10. In the summer of 1932 car 31 is about to reverse on Marine Terrace, Margate. Only one in three trams actually travelled on to Westbrook and the peak season service was the "Harbours" i.e. Ramsgate Harbour to Margate Seafront.
(National Tramway Museum. M.J.O'Connor)

11. Looking extremely smart in somewhat watery sunshine, car 15 pulls away along Marine Terrace.
(National Tramway Museum. M.J.O'Connor)

12. Only inches to spare...in this view one can well believe the old music hall joke about the novice motorist in the tall, thin car who tried to squeeze between two passing trams! Cars 56 and 58 are from the same batch, but they sport different style windscreens. The famous entertainment centre "Dreamland" is in the background. (D.W.K.Jones)

13. Shortly after the opening of the tramway in 1901 one of the original bogie cars hums along the seafront. (R.J.Harley Coll.)

14. The 1887 Jubilee Clock Tower erected in honour of Queen Victoria shows 12.23pm as a tram rounds the corner from Marine Drive. The centre pole is an electrical section feed carrying two cables of 500 volts DC which energised the overhead; similar section feeds were situated at half mile intervals. The goat cart in the foreground illustrates an earlier form of transport. Most of the well dressed visitors probably had lunch on their minds; for the less well off, the Shaftesbury House YMCA offered a cheap bed for the night. (R.J.Harley Coll.)

15. The young lady crossing the road in front of car 9 shows that hemlines have risen since the previous photo. Ladies' fashions have always had some influence on tramcar design, witness the height of entrance steps to accommodate "hobble" skirts and the decency boards screening the staircase and upper deck seats to prevent an immodest glimpse of a feminine ankle! As is usual for this era, a full load of passengers in their Sunday best passes towards Westbrook as a competing motor bus heads the other way. (R.J.Harley Coll.)

16. Woodruff the Jewellers has been in business since 1827. W.J.Woodruff, grandfather of the present owner L.T.Woodruff, was a keen amateur photographer and took this animated scene of the 1930s from the balcony of the shop

in 5 High Street. The East Kent bus on service 2 is a harbinger of the future for the trams. Soon the distinctive smell of the traction motors would be ousted by petrol and diesel fumes. (W.J.Woodruff)

17. An assorted collection of boats rides at anchor in this view taken before World War I. The crossover in front of the Albion can clearly be seen as the tracks divide in separate streets for the climb to Cliftonville. (R.J.Harley Coll.)

18. A mounted policeman talks to one of the char-a-banc drivers as car 56 accelerates towards the gradient by the Metropole Hotel. Some horse drawn excursions actually outlived the tramways and in the late 1930s one was still running between Ramsgate and Minster Tea Gardens. (R.J.Harley Coll.)

19. A gentleman stands idly in the roadway, his gaze fixed on car 13 which has just picked up passengers at a stop; from the look of the packed top deck, it would seem that some folk will have to forego the pleasures of a seat. (National Tramway Museum. M.N.A.Walker)

February 1918

20. Shortly after the tramway opened in 1901, car 14 in pristine condition prepares to tackle the grade of Fort Hill. The royal occasion being celebrated is probably the coronation of King Edward VII.
(National Tramway Museum. M.N.A.Walker)

Instructions to Conductors in cases of Dispute with Passengers.

In all cases of dispute the names and addresses of witnesses should be taken.

Refusing to pay fare on demand or to pay excess fare.—Obtain name and address and report.

Offering old silver or copper coin in payment of fare.—This must be refused, and a proper coin demanded. If passenger refuses to give a proper coin, obtain name and address.

Passenger offering bad money in payment of fare.—Coin must be kept quite apart from other money, and **in the presence of** passenger tested. If **bad,** and the passenger refuses to give good coin, obtain name and address.

Causing annoyance to passengers.—Obtain name and address.

Person in state of intoxication.—Should not be allowed to enter. If, however, found on the car or bus, should be ejected by the Conductor or under his direction.

Obstructing or interfering with the Conductor whilst in the execution of his duty.—Obtain names and addresses.

Refusing to SHOW TICKET when requested so to do, AND refusing name and address.—Refer the matter to an Inspector, or obtain assistance of police.

21. At the corner of King Street and The Parade, car 33 halts to pick up under the watchful eye of a member of the Margate constabulary, hands behind his back in classic policeman stance. Painters are hard at work giving surrounding buildings a pre-season face lift. (D.W.K.Jones)

Spitting or committing any other nuisance in or on the Car or Bus.—Obtain name and address.

Refusing to pay fare when entering the Car or Bus near the terminus, to secure a seat for return journey.—Obtain name and address.

Passenger doing wilful damage to the Department's property.—Obtain name and address.

Passenger refusing to put dog or other animal out of Car or Bus when asked to do so.—Conductor or some other person by his direction may remove it.

Passenger refusing to leave platforms or steps of the Car or Bus when requested so to do.—Obtain name and address.

Passenger smoking or carrying lighted pipe, cigar, or cigarette inside Car or Bus, or in front of the Trolley Pole Standard on the top of any Car, after being cautioned not to do so.—Obtain name and address.

Except in cases of assault, Conductors are not to give passengers into custody without the authority of an Inspector, Timekeeper, or other responsible Officer.

BY ORDER.

22. The descent of Fort Road, Margate was accomplished with great care by every motorman. Here the driver of car 34 concentrates on the approaching right angle bend at the bottom of the hill. (C.Carter)

23. Much of the property on Fort Hill has been demolished to make way for a dual carriageway road; this was still in the future as a tram ascends the interlaced track past the primitive semaphore signal for downhill cars. The sign on the traction standard actually reads "Downhill Cars Stop Here." Regulations permitted only one tram at a time to descend Fort Road; during inclement weather a company official was stationed with extra supplies of sand to strew on the rails as an aid to adhesion. (D.W.K.Jones)

CLIFTONVILLE

24. Fort Crescent leads towards Cliftonville and a number of elegant residences can be spied behind car 32 as it approaches the cross-over before the descent into Margate. (D.W.K.Jones)

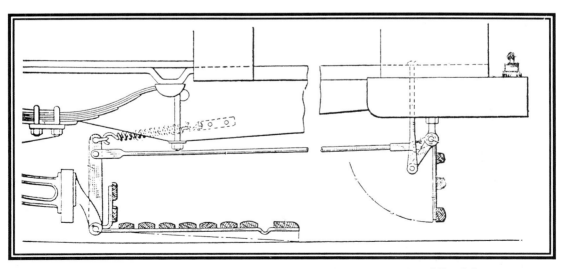

The lifeguard (known to some as the "cowcatcher"!) was designed so that people or objects striking the front gate would trigger a link to a drop tray in front of the wheels, thus being scooped up and avoiding injury. A reset button for the mechanism was located on the platform floor so that the motorman could act quickly.

25. A tram passes the same crossover as illustrated previously; this time the view is towards the pier.
(National Tramway Museum. R.B.Parr)

26. A driver leans out to watch the circus parade as he waits to enter the interlaced track in Fort Crescent. This postcard was sent in September 1911 when parades, variety shows on the pier, beach minstrels and concerts in the Fort bandstand to the right of the tram, were an accepted part of the season's entertainment. (R.J.Harley Coll.)

27. Car 14 is gently eased through the interlaced curve between Cliff Terrace and Fort
Crescent. (D.W.K.Jones)

28. On the corner of Cliff Terrace the passing
loop and interlaced track can clearly be seen.
This 1908 view is unusually deserted, however,
a lady is waiting for a tram at the stop opposite
County Stores. (R.J.Harley Coll.)

←

29. The sharp turn from Cliff Terrace into Athelstan Road is safely negotiated. (National Tramway Museum. M.J.O'Connor)

30. Athelstan Road, named after the Kentish hero who defeated the Danes in a naval battle in 851, links the seafront with the shopping centre of Cliftonville. Sunshine catches the conductor as he collects the fares on the top deck...not an easy task on a swaying tramcar, however, in this case the driver has slowed to walking pace for the facing points and sharp bend into Alexandra Road. (D.W.K.Jones)

31. The corner from Athelstan Road into
Alexandra Road is the setting for a fully loaded
car 54; such scenes were commonplace during
the summer months. (D.W.K.Jones)

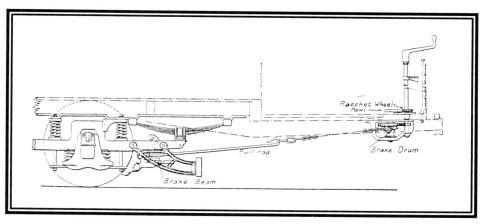

Hand brake linkage to truck and wheels

32. Although the headlight on car 39 had been moved to the dash some years previously, the advertisement for Robertson's Jams on the upper deck indicates the original position. (D.W.K.Jones)

33. A final view of Athelstan Road corner. Car 20 has just cleared the single track to let car 14 have right of way. No signals were necessary on this stretch as drivers relied on line of sight before proceeding. (D.W.K.Jones)

43A 0029

THE ISLE OF THANET ELECTRIC TRAMWAYS CO., LTD.

UP	FARE	DOWN
S. E. Station, Ramsgate, to York Street, Ramsgate	1D	Margate Jet. to Margate Hr.
Fagwell Road to Plains, Waterloo		Margate Station to Athelstan Rd. (Pettman's)
York Street, Ramsgate, to Thanet Road		Margate Hr. to Northdown corner
Thanet Road to Broadstairs Front		Athelstan Rd. to Wessish's
Broadstairs Front to Broadstairs Station		Northdown Corner to Tramy. Depot
Broadstairs Station to Tramy. Depot		Tramy. Depot to Broadstairs Station
Tramy. Depot to Northdown Corner		Broadstairs Station to Broadstairs Front
Wheatsheaf to Athelstan Rd		Broadstairs Front to Thanet Road
Northdown Cor. to King St. Margate		Thanet Road to York Street Ramsgate
Athelstan Rd. (Pettman's) to Margate Station		Plains, Waterloo to Peswell Road
Margate Hr. to Margate Jet.		York Street, Ramsgate, to S. E. Station Ramsgate

Issued subject to the Company's Bye-laws.

34. Looking along Alexandra Road in the early years of the century. At that time telephone wires were carried above the street, therefore the tramway company had to install guard wires to minimise the danger of a broken phone cable coming in contact with the 500 volt overhead. (R.J.Harley Coll.)

35. The white band on the traction standard next to car 20 indicated the presence of a section feed. The tram had to coast underneath and any application of power across the two overhead sections would have caused an electrical fireworks display from the trolley head. (G.L.Gundry Coll.)

36. The driver of car 3 has a few moments rest as he waits on the passing loop outside St. Pauls Church. (D.W.K.Jones)

HAND AND TRACK BRAKE ASSEMBLY

Wheel brake applied by handle *a*.

Turning the spiral cam *b*.

Attached to brake chain *c*.

Track brake applied by rotating handwheel *d*.

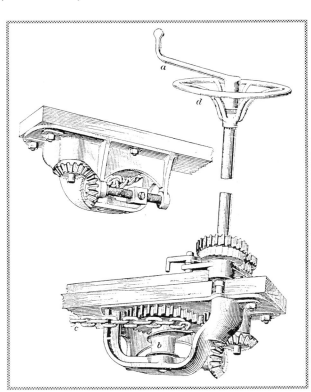

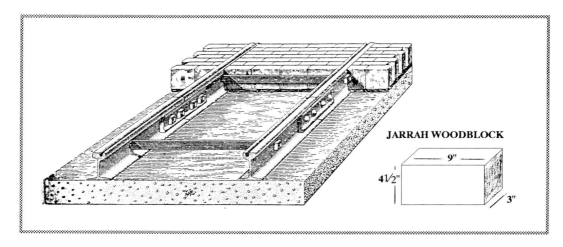

JARRAH WOODBLOCK

9"

4½"

3"

Woodblocks were made from Jarrah hardwood. They were dropped in pitch then grouted in position with a mixture of sand and cement. Rails rested on a firm six inch Portland cement base.

37. Clearly shown in this early scene is the woodblock paving outside St. Paul's Church. The tramway company was obliged by law to maintain the road surface to a distance of 18 ins. from the outer rail. Notice the change of paving at the gas lamp. (G.L.Gundry Coll.)

38. Past the church there was a section of single track; car 43 travels along this part of Northdown Road. Just in front of the tram are the points leading to the curious double/single track featured in the next view. (D.W.K.Jones)

39. Narrow spacing between double tracks meant that two trams could not pass. Hopefully car 13 will not live up to its unlucky number and meet a tram going the other way! (C.Carter)

40. An inspector hops aboard to join the motorman on the front platform before the tram veers to the left of the photograph; it will then enter private right of way to begin the cross country journey to St. Peter's and Broadstairs. (C.Carter)

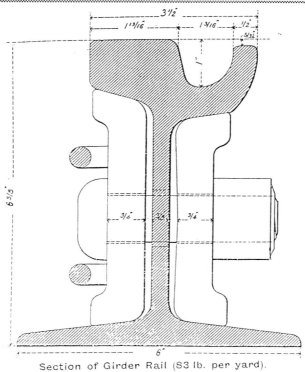

Section of Girder Rail (83 lb. per yard).

KENTISH WOODS AND FIELDS

41. Towards the end of tramway operation late
afternoon shadows frame car 35 as it takes the
curve onto the reserved tracks a few yards
further on from the previous view.
(D.W.K.Jones)

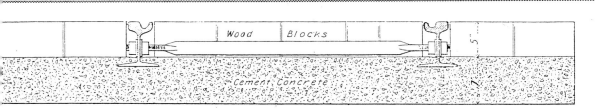

Section of Permanent Way (Single Track) with Wood Paving.

42. Car 13 heads along tree lined reserved
track towards Northdown Park Road.
(D.W.K.Jones)

43. A dull day in summer on the reserved track short cut between Northdown Park and Northdown Road. The only other signs of habitation are the farmers' sheds dotted about the landscape. (D.W.K.Jones)

44. On the pole at the corner of Northdown Park Road and the reserved track is affixed a notice.."Private Road Unadopted." You can almost hear the sighs of..'and about time too!' from the knot of waiting people as "junior" spies an approaching westbound car for Margate. The top deck passengers on car 8 look on sympathetically as they pull away in the direction of Broadstairs. (D.W.K.Jones)

45. All clear ahead, car 33 sways past Laleham Road. Already in the background is a sign detailing building land for sale. Very much an omen for the future at this location. (D.W.K.Jones)

46. Further along Northdown Park Road car 53 brushes past hedgerows as the motorman increases speed on this straight section of track. (National Tramway Museum)

47. Where was the romance of the tram to be found? In grim, industrial streets or here, outside the Wheatsheaf Inn amongst the oaks and the elms of the Kentish countryside? (National Tramway Museum. R.B.Parr.)

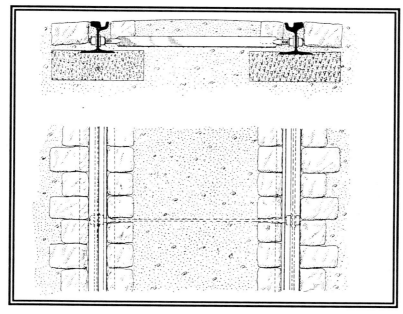

THANET RESERVED TRACK FORMATION

48. Beyond the Wheatsheaf two trams pass in a truly Arcadian setting. They add a note of colour in their bright crimson red and off-white livery against the bare branches and the clear blue early spring sky. The time is the mid 1930s; soon such scenes would be just a memory. (National Tramway Museum)

49. A few houses were clustered at Northdown Hill, but there was little other development as car 8 hugs the side of the lane on its way to Cliftonville. (D.W.K.Jones)

50. In the mid 1930s the housing boom had started and lines of the well known British "semis" stretch across the horizon in this view taken outside the depot in St. Peter's. Soon both the tram and the fields would be gone for good. (D.W.K.Jones)

51. Looking splendid, the brand new trams assemble outside the depot for the launch of the interurban transport system. The date is 1901 and it was a proud moment for all concerned. (National Tramway Museum)

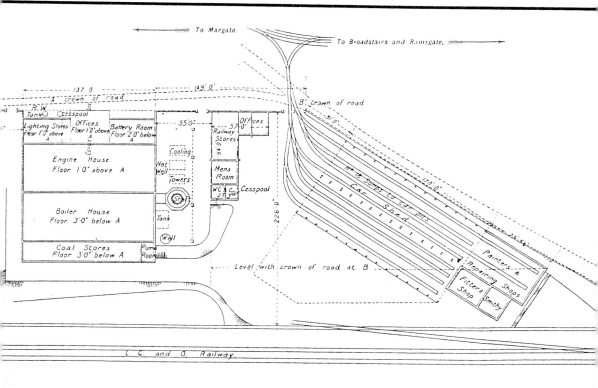

52. The pre-opening press celebrations continued with a look inside the sheds where the fleet, in its rich maroon and primrose livery, was arranged in neat lines above the inspection pits. (National Tramway Museum)

53. In the early 1930's the depot yard took on a less glamorous appearance as the clutter of old trams increased. Noteworthy in this view is the single deck water car 61 which we shall meet again in the rolling stock section. (National Tramway Museum. A.G.Jenson)

←

54. Inside the depot, unseen by the general public, the important business of repairing and renovating the fleet was carried on. In the background are the belt driven lathes and drill presses and in front of the tram is a very home made looking stove and chimney pipe. (D.W.K.Jones)

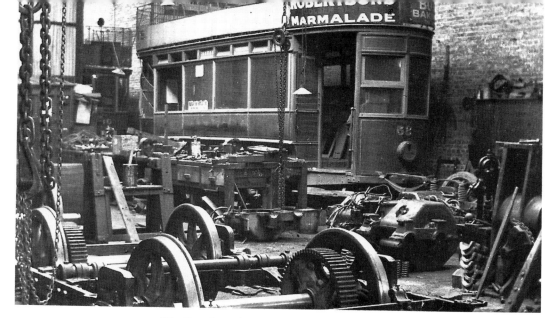

55. Car 52 waits to be rebuilt, surrounded by trucks, wheels and motors. In the tramway era very little was wasted and most metal and wooden tramcar parts could be either recycled or repaired. (D.W.K.Jones)

56. The small, but dedicated staff at St. Peter's depot performed miracles of reconstruction. Here we see the staircase of car 38 in front of another tram which is receiving a new dash and windscreen. In this way the company avoided the extra expense of replacing the older vehicles with new rolling stock. Note the suspended upper deck structure. (D.W.K.Jones)

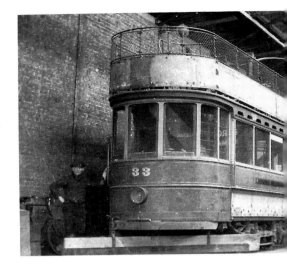

57. Although the winds around Thanet can be pretty keen in winter, snow and blizzards are not a regular occurrence. The trams had a good reputation for getting through whatever the weather, hence the snow plough on car 33 just in case it was needed. (D.W.K.Jones)

58. A view known to many tramway enthusiasts is this one of car 25 crossing the single track on St. Peter's railway bridge. Perhaps the driver of AKO 92 would concur with the sentiments of the local motoring correspondent in the 1935 article. However, most people at that time could not afford a motor car and they relied upon public transport. The tram itself carries an advertisement for Munro Cobbs, the letters are green on a cream background. Forthcoming local events were displayed in red letters on paper stickers affixed to the fenders of the trams. (D.W.K.Jones)

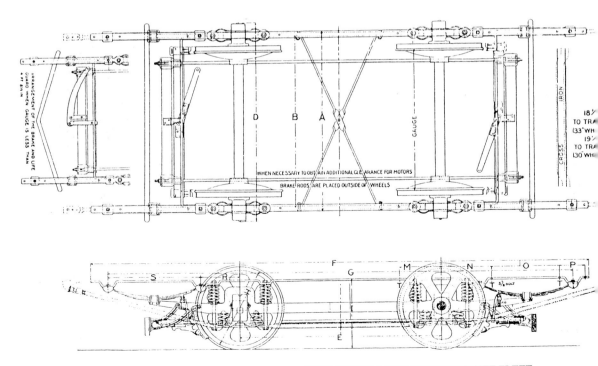

STANDARD BRILL 21E TRUCK AS USED UNDER MOST OF THE THANET FLEET

BROADSTAIRS TOP ROAD

1935 MOTORING ARTICLE

MOTORING

The tramways are an undoubted nuisance, not to say danger. In Ramsgate, Broadstairs and Margate the motorist should regard them with caution as in many places the change from single to double track entails a sudden swerve on the part of a tram, which does not always leave room for a car between it and the kerb. On either side of Broadstairs, too, are special tramway tracks which at first glance might well be mistaken for ordinary roads in execrable condition. Motorists are forbidden to use these thoroughfares; and it is safe to say that any motorist who has once unwittingly disobeyed the rules will not easily be tempted to do so again.

59. The Top Road service was a by-pass line linking Broadstairs and Ramsgate Harbour avoiding the narrow, winding descent into Broadstairs centre. Passenger levels were poor and the section was normally worked by one car from the 41-50 series. Car 45, seen at the depot, has been converted to one man operation; the staircases have been removed and the entrances reversed. The seats on the top deck were left, presumably waiting for some aspiring mountaineers to scale the heights and occupy them! (C.Carter)

60. Before the main line through Broadstairs centre was in use, a fully loaded tram noses out of Osborne Road at the future terminus of the Top Road service. The photographer is standing on the route of the former horse tramway which had such a short existence.
(National Tramway Museum)

61. Car 45 pictured at the corner of St. Peter's Park Road and Broadstairs High Street. By this time common sense had prevailed and the top deck, seats and all, had gone.
(G.L.Gundry)

62. Latterly car 44 took over the Top Road shuttle service and in 1936 it featured in an article headed, "England's Oldest Tram Driver." Mr. W. Walsh of Westover Road, St. Peter's, aged 78, claimed to have driven some 350,000 miles in his career at Thanet. Mr. Walsh went on to say that car 44 was his favourite tram. (G.L.Gundry)

63. Out on the Top Road there was normally plenty of time to pose for a photograph, the stretch along Salisbury Avenue was private track and the other roads contained very little traffic. Maybe it was because of this that a number of unofficial speed records were set here; one driver Bill Tattersall was quoted as regularly driving "in excess of 50 miles per hour." What the passengers, if any, thought about it, has not been recorded. (D.W.K.Jones)

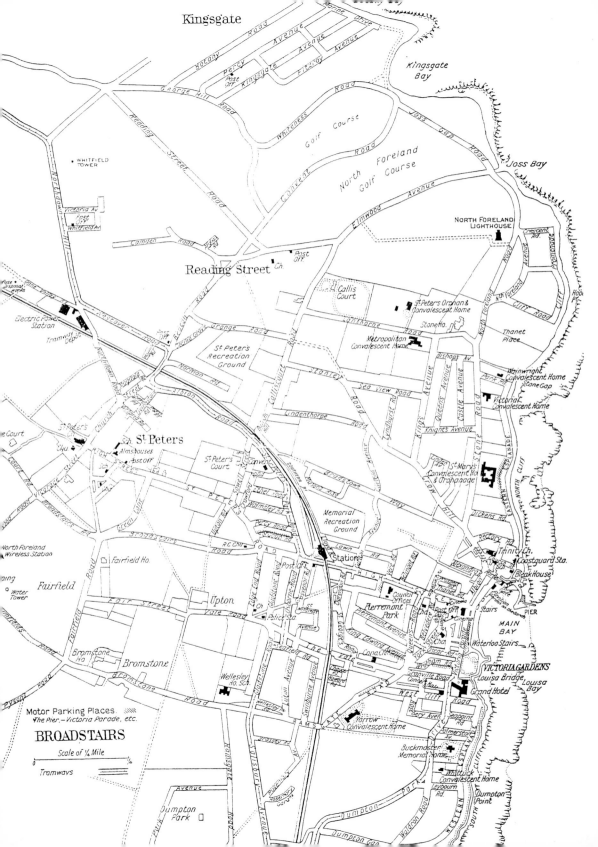

64. On the hills above Broadstairs at the junction of the Top Road and the main line, car 49 pauses as the points are changed. One wonders whether the animals immortalised by Charles Dickens in the Trotwood donkey fights had once grazed on these downs. Most of "David Copperfield" was written in Broadstairs and the author knew the area well. (D.W.K.Jones)

CROSS SECTION OF CLAMP AND WIRE

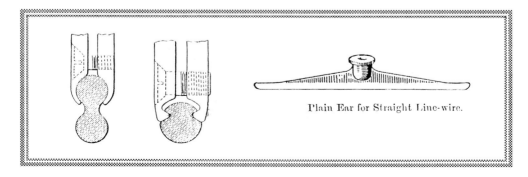

Plain Ear for Straight Line-wire.

BROADSTAIRS MAIN LINE

65. On 5th May 1901 the railway bridge at Broadstairs was replaced to allow the passage of trams and the carriageway also had to be lowered. Here car 59 passes under the warning notice instructing passengers to keep their seats. (C.Carter)

66. Car 21 bound for Margate prepares to disappear down the dip under Broadstairs railway bridge; behind the tram is the symmetrical passing loop opposite Clarendon Road. The chap standing on the top deck had better sit down quickly as he is in imminent danger of conducting a test on the insulating properties of his hat as it comes in contact with the 500 volt overhead slung under the bridge. No doubt he was being chivalrous in offering his seat to a lady and didn't intend an electrifying finale! (D.W.K.Jones)

67. On first sight it seems from this postcard of the High Street in Broadstairs that the photographer has erased the tram rails. However, closer inspection will reveal that the tram has emerged from Queens Road which is to the left of the picture. (G.L.Gundry Coll.)

Queens Road   Broadstairs

68. Queens Road lies on a falling gradient towards the sea; car 44 is pictured surrounded by children eager to have their likeness recorded for posterity. There was more time in those days to stand and stare. (G.L.Gundry Coll.)

69. A couple of top deck passengers cast glances over the sea, as their tram halts on Broadstairs Esplanade. The driver is out of uniform and one can only assume that he may be a retired employee who has come back in high season to help out. Notice also the side indicator slip board on the rocker panel; on some trams it was fixed on the maroon waist panel instead. (G.L.Gundry)

70. The Thanet trams had character, a quality the replacing buses never possessed. Here car 18 rolls along the broad sweep of reserved track outside Broadstairs. The lady on the top deck has a marvellous view of the chalk hills and the coast. (National Tramway Museum)

71. Accidents bring out the crowds. On 27th
May 1905 car 47 went out of control on Belle
Vue Road, Ramsgate; it gathered speed,
jumped the rails and crashed into a grocer's
shop. A seven year old girl in the shop was
seriously injured.
(National Tramway Museum)

72. The side view shows more of the damage
to the front and the staircase. Note the curtains
which added a suitably Edwardian touch to the
lower saloon. Purists of the English language
may object to the American spelling of
"Harbour" on the side destination board. A
plausible explanation is that the first 40 trams
were shipped over in crated parts from the St.
Louis Car Company and one must assume that
destination equipment was included in the
order. (National Tramway Museum)

73. First shore up your building then remove
your tramcar! The instructions to the foreman
probably contained this advice. After the
accident car 47 was removed in disgrace to
await rebuilding at the depot; obviously the
repairers weren't superstitious because it was
patched up with parts from car 41 which went
over the cliff at Madeira Walk. The rebuilt car

emerged from the works and on its first journey
promptly ran away down Broadstairs High
Street, colliding with a coal lorry. Legend hath
it that for many years afterwards no sane
motorman would go near the tram and it was
never used in service on Friday the thirteenth!
(R.J.Harley Coll.)

WELLINGTON CRESCENT

74. The seafront was reached via Plains of Waterloo clearly seen here as the gap in the elegant architectural sweep of Wellington Crescent. (G.L.Gundry Coll.)

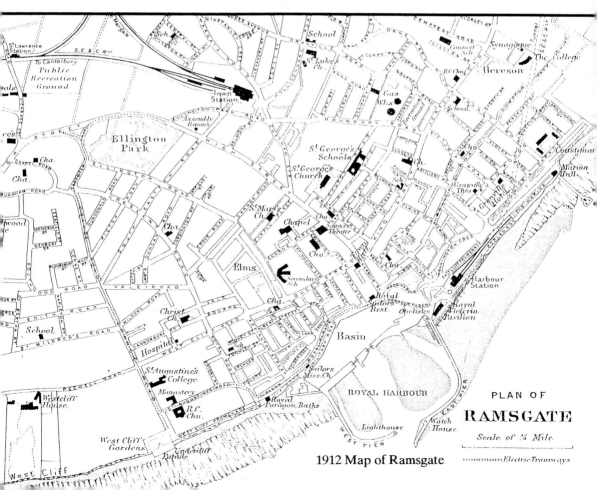

1912 Map of Ramsgate

PLAN OF

RAMSGATE

Scale of ¼ Mile

ˈˈˈˈˈˈˈˈˈˈˈˈ Electric Tramways

37S 8984

THE ISLE OF THANET
ELECTRIC SUPPLY Co., LTD.

UP	FARE	DOWN
1		16
2		15
3		14
4	**1D**	13
5		12
6		11
7		10
8		9
9		8
10		7
11		6
12		5
13		4
14		3
15		2
16		1

For Stage Numbers See Fare Bills.

TICKET TO BE SHOWN ON DEMAND.

For Stage Numbers See Fare Bills.

Bell Punch Co. Uxbridge. 11-27

75. Stirring images of the Napoleonic Wars are conjured up by the street names here-abouts, these are reinforced by the artillery piece at the end of Wellington Crescent. Some conductors used to tell passengers that it was there to see off bus competition!
(National Tramway Museum)

MADEIRA WALK

76. The series of sharp bends on the steep gradient of Madeira Walk made this location one of the wonders of the tramway world. A car is seen here edging its way down to Ramsgate Harbour; the gentleman with the umbrella standing to the left of the tram is at the spot where car 41 came to grief some years previously. (R.J.Harley Coll.)

77. The tiered effect of the roads on the other side of the harbour can clearly be seen in the background as one of the original four wheel cars negotiates the bend. The curves here were eased somewhat after the 1905 accident. (R.J.Harley Coll.)

78. The town council feared for the reputation of Ramsgate when on 3rd August 1905 yet another tram mishap made the news. This postcard is dated 24th August 1905, just three weeks after the event and the people are busy peering over the precipice at the wreckage. (G.L.Gundry Coll.)

79. At the bottom of the cliff car 41 lies on its side; for all those who make models of trams, the top deck seating layout should be of interest. The policeman was stationed to prevent souvenir hunters. (G.L.Gundry Coll.)

80. Miraculously the only injury of note was to the motorman who jumped off before the 32ft drop and fell on his head. Certain unkind speculation at the time suggested that where there was no sense there was no feeling and the driver was blamed for failing to control his car as it skidded on the wet rails. Car 41 was damaged beyond repair, but as noted before, some parts were salvaged to mend car 47 the victim of the May accident. (R.J.Harley Coll.)

81. Looking from a different angle towards the
Royal Victoria Pavilion one of the narrow cars
of the 41-50 batch descends the hill.
(G.L.Gundry Coll.)

82. Problems arose with eight wheel cars
shortly after their entry into service. The main
fault was the tendency of the bogies to derail
and the company took the unusual step of
shortening each car body and placing it on a
four wheel truck. Not surprisingly views of
these trams in original condition are rare; here
we see one of the bogie cars ascending the hill
with paper destination stickers in the two
central lower saloon windows. One was
lettered "S.E.Station Ramsgate" and the other
"Westbrook Margate." (R.J.Harley Coll.)

83. Car 23 shows all the elegance of late Victorian tramway style as it rides sedately down Madeira Walk. At the turn of the century it was extremely rare for British trams to come equipped with windscreen protection; the Thanet company were obviously mindful of the welfare of the motorman and the conductor. (G.L.Gundry Coll.)

Trolley Mast as originally fitted to the Isle of Thanet trams. A cover was subsequently fixed to the top of the mast to prevent ingress of rainwater.

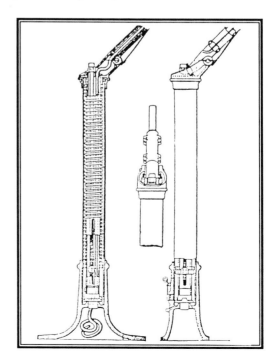

84. Right up to the end of operation the cars were neatly turned out, as can be seen in this 1930s view on the lower section of Madeira Walk. (W.J.Haynes)

85. Single deck car 45 has reversed at the harbour crossover and is climbing the hill back to Broadstairs via the Top Road in this scene from summer of 1922. George Gundry took this photo after riding on the tram and alighting at the Harbour; the car then reversed quickly on the crossover and did not wait on the quayside siding for a layover period. (G.L.Gundry)

86. At the bottom of this interesting section of tramway there is yet another set of curves to be negotiated. (R.J.Harley Coll.)

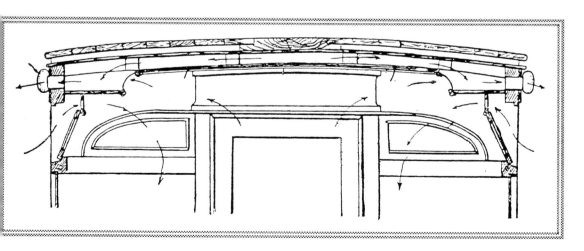

Ventilation Of Car Roof.

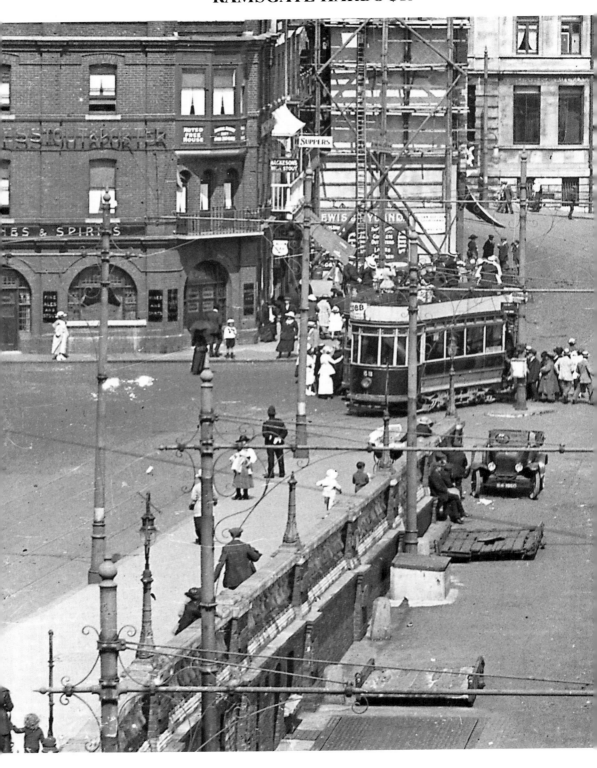

87. On the quayside opposite York Street a tram does good business in this picture of past transport glories; the fishing boats, the old motor cars and the tramway have all been casualties of so called progress. (R.J.Harley Coll.)

88. Car 46, probably on the Top Road service, waits on the siding as the conductor adjusts the trolley rope. (D.W.K.Jones)

3E 6452

THE ISLE OF THANET
ELECTRIC SUPPLY CO., LD.

UP	FARE	DOWN
1		14
2		13
3	$2\frac{1}{2}$d	12
4		11
5		10
6		9
7		8
8		7
9		6
10		5
11		4
12		3
13		2
14		1

For Stage No. See Fare Bill. — Ticket to be shown on demand. — For Stage No. See Fare Bill.

Bell Punch Co., Uxbridge. 11-27

Swivel Head Trolley.

89. A scene redolent of the early Edwardian era. Two ladies with parasols cross in front of car 43 which boasts its first and least attractive windscreen. This tram was actually working a main line service and as the front indicator boards suggest its route was via Broadstairs seafront. (R.J.Harley Coll.)

90. The combination of tramcars, sailing boats and the local architecture is aesthetically pleasing. Car 47 is in the siding situated in Military Road, whilst car 27 stops to pick up on its journey along Royal Parade towards the station. An official of the company is poised with a spade to clean out the point blade on the crossover. (R.J.Harley Coll.)

The terminal siding is on the left while the LCDR teminus is on the right. This was the location of more than one runaway train crash - see *Sittingbourne to Ramsgate* (Middleton Press).

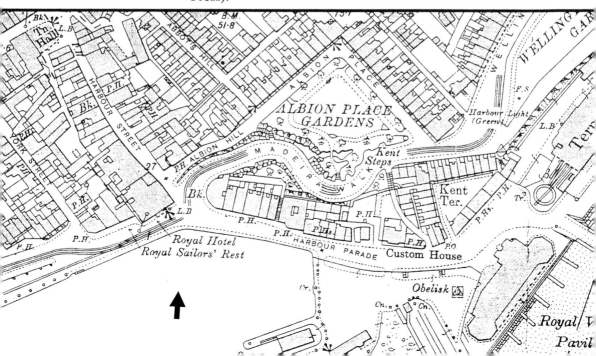

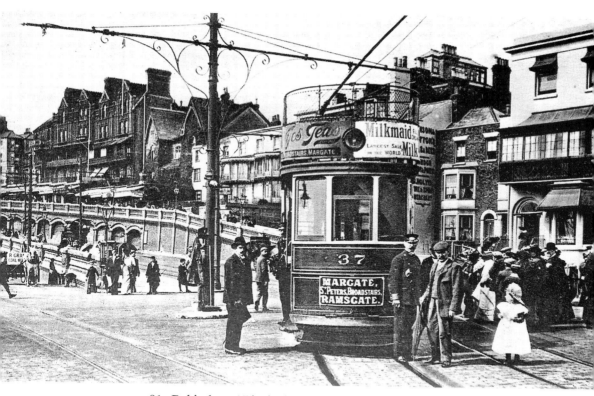

91. Behind car 37 is the largest centre pole on the system, and to the left can be glimpsed the coalman's cart. The tramway continues to the town on the lower inclined road, to the right of the cart. (R.J.Harley Coll.)

From a trackwork construction manual 1905.
STANDARD TRAILING CROSSOVER
Note: The track gauge at Thanet was 3' 6".

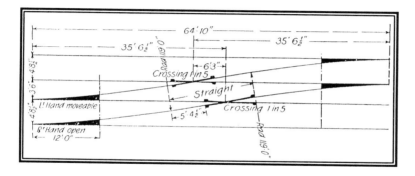

92. Hill climbing was all in a day's work for the efficient Thanet system. Here car 2 makes headway up Royal Parade with the arches as an elegant backdrop. (R.J.Harley Coll.)

93. Behind car 27 is St. Augustine's Church designed and financed by the famous architect E. Welby Pugin and often referred to as "Pugin's Gem" reflecting the master's finest work. The late Poet Laureat, Sir John Betjeman was an admirer of the church and acknowledging the fact that tramways were also one of his loves, he commented that in this part of Ramsgate, the setting offered a rare combination of beauty. (R.J.Harley Coll.)

STATION TERMINUS

94. After a brief journey through the streets of Ramsgate, the trams turned off Ellington Park Road to enter private track on the forecourt of the old Ramsgate Town station. (D.W.K.Jones)

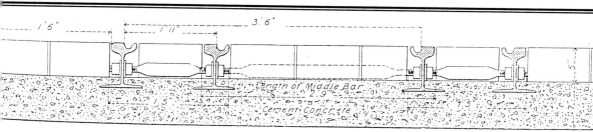

Section of Permanent Way Showing Interlacing Lines.

95. The lady in black with her trusty "brolly" is a reminder that not all Dickensian characters perished with their creator, and that even on a summer's day in 1922, such eccentrics were still about. The party leaving the station building are just about to miss the tram as will be shown in the next photograph. (G.L.Gundry)

96. Car 58 has just arrived at the terminus and the conductor turns the trolley. Notice that one staircase is used for unloading whilst the same three passengers from the previous view are waiting to board at the other end. (G.L.Gundry)

97. The Southern Railway rerouted and closed
some of the railway lines in 1926. Consequently
the original station was demolished and the
site cleared. Here we see car 22 at the end of
the line, terminating rather uselessly on an
empty, derelict lot. Shortly afterwards this
section of tramway was given up and the
terminus was moved to the High Street.
(National Tramway Museum)

ROLLING STOCK

98. Looking splendid after its repaint, car 9 is in substantially original condition and it is still equipped with the St. Louis frame truck which was not used anywhere else in Great Britain. They were described as hard wearing and reliable, but they gave a very robust ride for the passengers! (D.W.K.Jones)

CARS 1-20. Built in 1900 and supplied in 1901. Bodies by St. Louis Car Company, U.S.A. and trucks were of the cast frame type by the same company; they were four wheel and of six feet wheel base.

CARS 21-40. Details as 1-20, except that they had bogies which were of the St. Louis reversed type 13, with a wheel base of four feet.

CARS 41-50. Built in 1901 by G.F.Milnes and supplied on Brill 21E four wheel trucks of six feet wheel base.

CARS 51-60. Built in 1903 by British Electric Car Company on Brill 21E trucks as cars 41-50.

CAR 61. The works car. This was home made and mounted on a Brush "Aa" six-feet wheel base truck.

Nearly all cars were extensively rebuilt during their lives at Thanet. Alterations included repositioning of headlights, removal of the waist rail on the dash, installation of new windscreens and much minor work concerning seating and interior arrangements. The original livery was rich maroon and primrose, with the maroon panels lined in gold. The crest carried on the waist panel was a display of the coats of arms of Margate, Broadstairs and Ramsgate. In 1927 as cars were reconditioned they appeared in a brighter livery of light crimson red lined in yellow and the window frames, rocker panels, upper deck panels and windscreens were painted off-white with black lining on the rocker panel. MARGATE BROADSTAIRS RAMSGATE were in black lettering on the rocker panel. The fleet number was gold shaded blue and the trucks and lifeguards were painted oxide brown; trolley masts, handrails, fenders and controllers were black. Some trams after World War I were painted sage green and ivory as a temporary measure until a full repaint in red.

◀

99. Car 1 is seen here in St. Peter's depot in its final condition having received a new truck; this last livery with the town crests on the waist panel demonstrates the pride of the coach painters in a really smart job. (D.W.K.Jones)

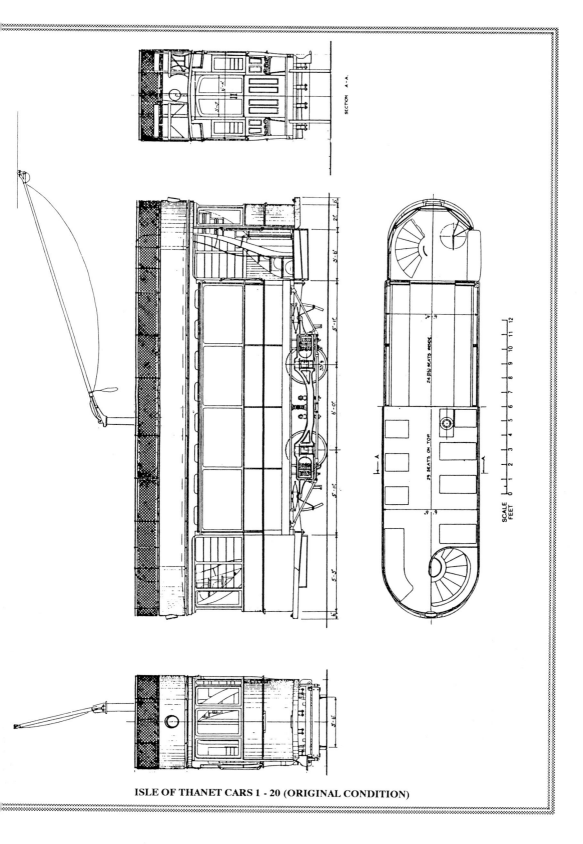

ISLE OF THANET CARS 1 - 20 (ORIGINAL CONDITION)

100. On a publicity run before the start of the system, one of the splendid eight wheel cars poses with passengers who seem to have been rounded up from the local boys' home. In 1901 the locals must surely have been very proud of their new trams. (G.L.Gundry Coll.)

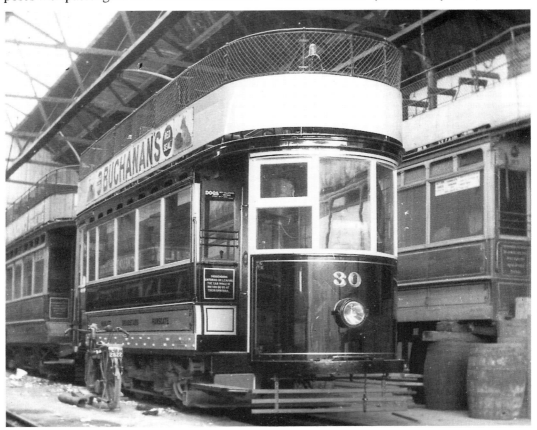

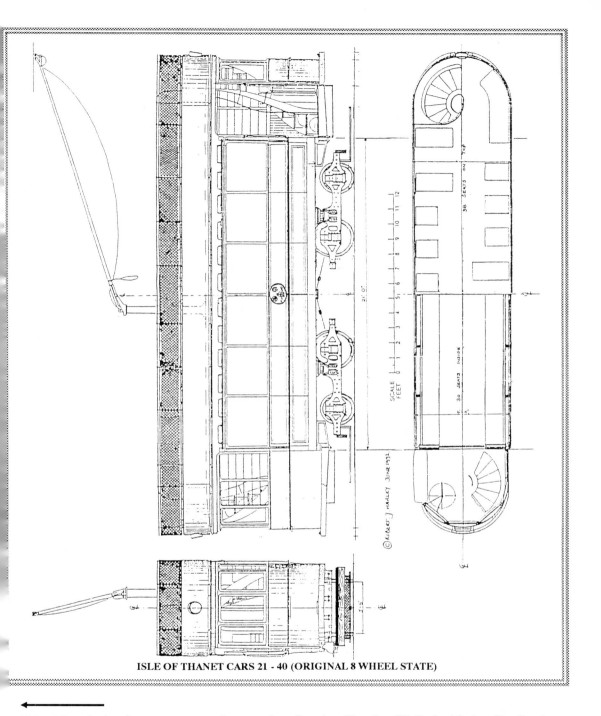

ISLE OF THANET CARS 21 - 40 (ORIGINAL 8 WHEEL STATE)

101. After the bogie cars were cut down and retrucked they were one of the mainstays of the fleet. Notice the condition of the tram and the two notices in white letters on the front bulkhead; these read ....*Dogs Not Allowed On Car Except On A Lead*.... and below the bulkhead window ....*Passengers Entering Or Leaving The Car While In Motion Do So At Their Own Risk*. Also of note to the left of the tram is the antique motor bicycle with the London registration LY 2822. The most probable explanation is that it belonged to one of the fitters, and was not there for a service at the company's expense! (D.W.K.Jones)

102. The "narrow" cars in the batch 41-50 were very similar to a number of trams delivered to the other side of the county at Chatham. It soon became apparent that they were not large enough to cope with the traffic demands in Thanet. Here is car 44. in almost original state with lattice gates and open platforms. (R.J.Harley Coll.)

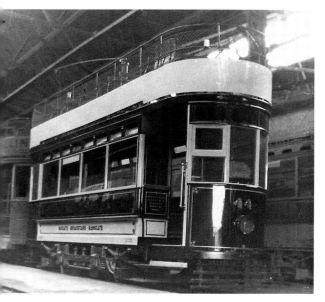

103. In its last reincarnation car 44 is seen here at the depot awaiting its turn to take up service on the Top Road. (D.W.K.Jones)

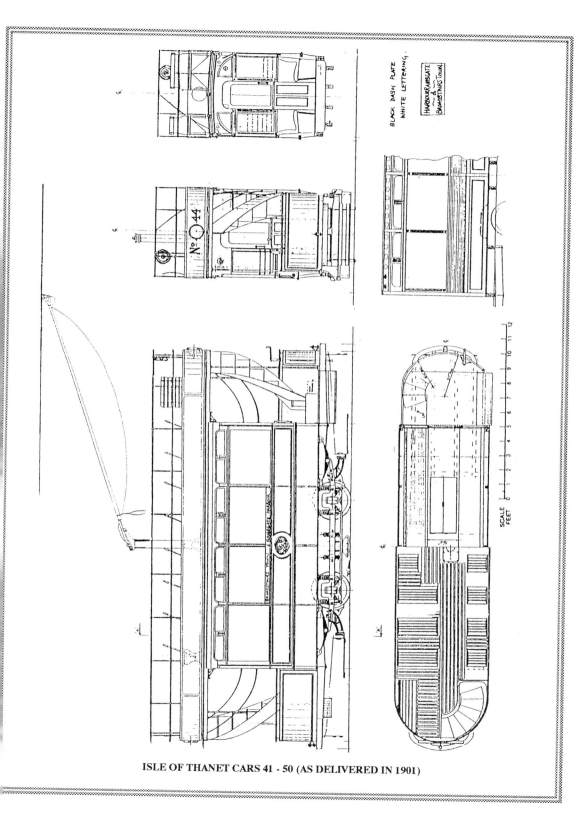

BLACK DASH PLATE
WHITE LETTERING.

HARBOUR, RAMSGATE
&
BROADSTAIRS TOWN.

N° 44

SCALE
FEET 0 1 2 3 4 5 6 7 8 9 10 11 12

ISLE OF THANET CARS 41 - 50 (AS DELIVERED IN 1901)

104. A fine view of cut down car 45 on the depot siding at St. Peter's. This trim little vehicle had a fair turn of speed and as can be seen by the reversed entrances, was operated by only one crew member. In front of the car some lengths of rail are mounted on two jockey bogies, small four wheel trucks designed to be used in emergencies when a car axle broke. They could then be inserted under a disabled car to get it back to the depot for attention. Here their use is confined to helping the permanent way department transport materials. At night, track repairs would be carried out after normal service had finished, replacement rails being be towed out on these bogies behind the works car. (D.W.K.Jones)

105. The late Walter Gratwicke who was one of Britain's foremost authorities on tramways, once described the British Electric Car Co. as the premier cheapjack car builder. It is a tribute to the maintenance and repair skills at St. Peter's that cars 51-60 lasted so long and as is obvious from this photo of car 53, that their overall condition was excellent right up to the mid 1930's. (D.W.K.Jones)

106. The lower saloon interior of car 53 has the stark simplicity of longitudinal seating. Different varieties of hard wood show up in lighter tones in the bulkhead panels and bench seat backs. The 75 minute ride between the two termini no doubt encouraged "good posture", so beloved of our forebears, but it couldn't have been very comfortable. Note also the tinted bulkhead windows to prevent windscreen glare at night and the slatted floor with inspection hatches, one for each motor.
(D.W.K.Jones)

107. An interesting close-up of the platform of car 53 with the handbrake handle with the pawl and ratchet at the base. The side route boards are stored in the windscreen window opposite the entrance step; in the lower saloon a paper sticker advertises a return fare of tenpence (4p) between Margate and Ramsgate!
(D.W.K.Jones)

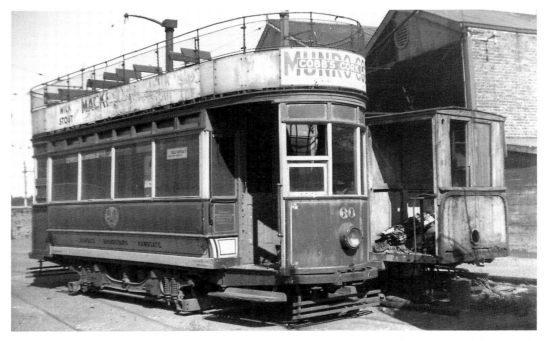

108. Car 60 was latterly retrucked on an old St. Louis frame from one of the early trams. It was then relegated to works shunter and permanent way car, whilst the purpose-built works car 61, seen next to it, rusted away. (D.W.K.Jones)

109. Car 61 could almost be described as a box on wheels, but it served its purpose as a water car and maid of all work until old age overtook it. It was painted in the same maroon and cream as the passenger cars and it is seen here at the depot resting alongside an open goods wagon with a primitive screw down brake next to the coupling rod. (C.Carter)

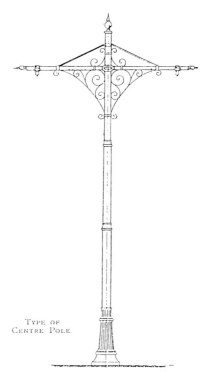

TYPE OF
CENTRE POLE.

TROUBLE AT WESTBROOK

110. Incidents on the road were rare and it is true to say that the trams were very reliable. However, even in the best families things can go amiss, as is apparent with car 15 which has a broken axle. The repair team are seen jacking up the tram ready to slide under a four-wheel jockey bogie so that the vehicle can be removed from the terminus. (D.W.K.Jones)

111. Car 15 is now seen perched at a rather ungainly angle ready to be towed away to St. Peter's; thus with a minimum of disruption the service has been resumed. (D.W.K.Jones)

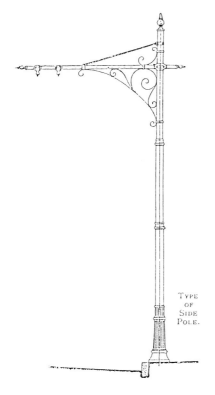

TYPE
OF
SIDE
POLE.

OVERHEAD

112. A fine view from the top deck of one of the 21-40 series cars illustrates the trolley pole and mast with the box like cover to prevent ingress of rain water. Single and double arm suspension hangers can be seen supporting the overhead at Ramsgate harbour. (D.W.K.Jones)

113. In this view of Margate seafront the traction standard with the white band carrying the feeder cables can clearly be seen. Next to it is the section box or feeder pillar which contained switches so that each half mile section either side could be electrically isolated in case of emergency. The ball and spike finial on top of the standard was devised as an ornament and as a deterrent offering a not very comfortable perch for any passing bird. (R.J.Harley Coll.)

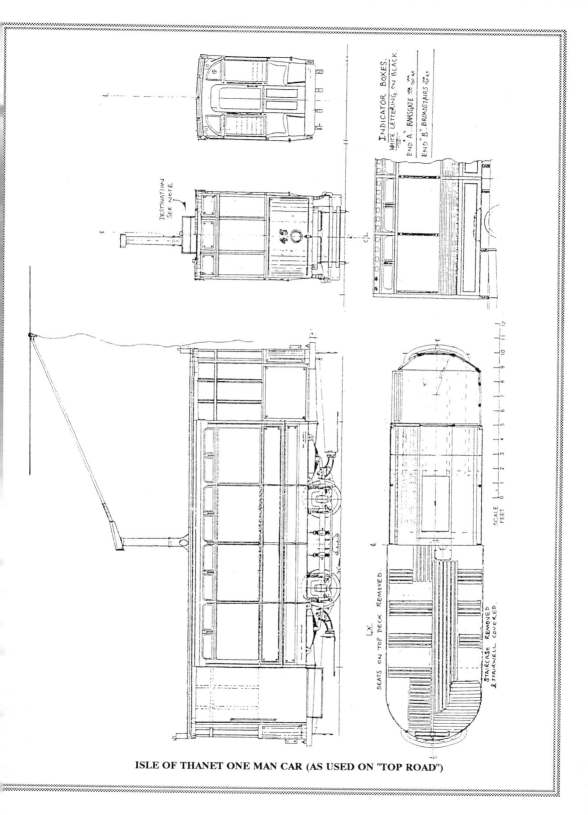

INDICATOR BOXES.
WHITE LETTERING ON BLACK.
END "A" RAMSGATE ¼ᴵᴺ TOP ¾ᴵᴺ
END "B" BROADSTAIRS ¼ᴵᴺ TOP ¾ᴵᴺ

DESTINATION SEE NOTE

DESTINATION SEE NOTE

45

C/L

SEATS ON TOP DECK REMOVED.

STAIRCASE REMOVED
& STAIRWELL COVERED.

SCALE FEET 0 1 2 3 4 5 6 7 8 9 10 11 12

ISLE OF THANET ONE MAN CAR (AS USED ON "TOP ROAD")

114. The details of the swivel head trolley and the trolley pole are revealed in this photo at Westbrook. Swivel head trolleys allowed a greater range of movement which meant that the overhead wires did not have to be hung over the centre of each track. This was important in avoiding an ugly mesh of wires; bracket arms were decorated with scroll work and could carry the overhead discreetly at the side of the road thus leaving an open skyline. (D.W.K.Jones)

115. Earlier in the book a circus parade in Margate was featured. Here is the company's own high wire act arrayed for the camera outside St. Peter's depot. In the event of a breakage in the overhead this group was called out with cutting and splicing equipment to effect the necessary repairs. In the winter it could not have been pleasant exposed to the elements some twenty feet above the roadway, with the added danger of ensuring that no current was earthed as the brave linesmen tackled the 500 volts plus in the overhead. (D.W.K.Jones)

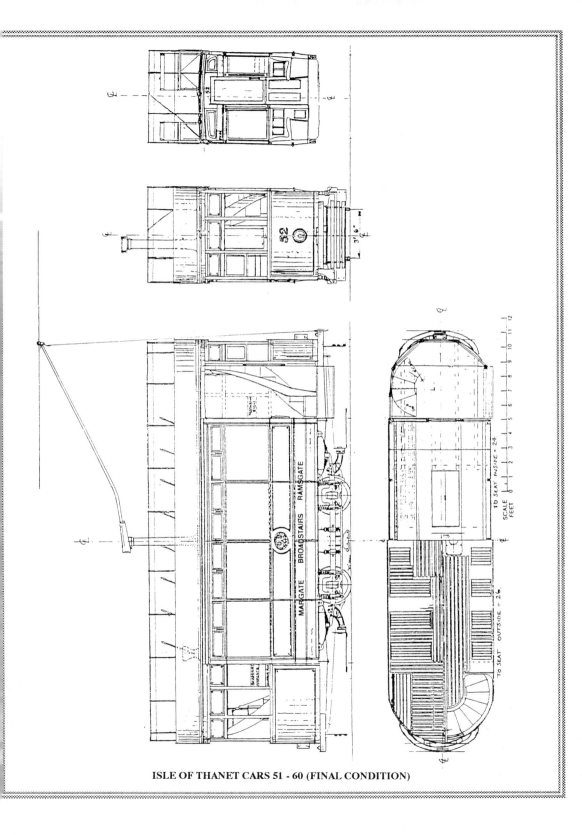

ISLE OF THANET CARS 51 - 60 (FINAL CONDITION)

TRACKWORK

116. Track renewal takes place in Margate and the rails, tie bars and fishplates are laid on a solid concrete base. The service has been revised until the new layout is completed; car 4 passes a model T Ford parked at the kerb, whilst another tram in the background prepares to turn into King Street wrong road working as far as the top of Fort Hill. (D.W.K.Jones)

117. The double/single track in Northdown Road with car 31 heading for Broadstairs. Why this layout was adopted instead of the more normal single or interlaced track is a mystery. Obviously there was a saving on points and crossings, but it was still impossible for two trams to pass without a collision. (D.W.K.Jones)

118. On private right of way and out of town sections the company used a simpler track formation as illustrated in the picture of car 20 on the Northdown reserved track. Basically each rail rested on a series of concrete blocks laid lengthways with the rest of the roadway paved with macadam. A toothed row of granite setts gave extra support on either side of the rails. (D.W.K.Jones)

119. At the eastern end of Fort Crescent inter-laced track was employed as is shown in this view. Some tramway operators in Britain used this method extensively, one presumes to save on points, whilst others preferred single track where the carriageway narrowed. The interlaced curve at the end of the crescent is pictured in more detail in photo 27.
(D.W.K.Jones)

STAFF

120. No organisation can run effectively without committed staff and the Isle of Thanet was fortunate in the men they employed. The first manager Mr. Humphries left in 1907 to be replaced by J.A.Forde who stayed until the closure. Under the latter's management staff relations were particularly good and a friendly atmosphere was noted by many visitors who came to St. Peter's depot. The abandonment of the tramways brought misery to many who found their skills on the scrap heap with their former charges. Men who were sacked without pension rights experienced great hardship; this human tragedy is often overlooked by transport historians who glibly record that the Isle of Thanet trams were replaced by East Kent buses on Wednesday 24th March 1937, without telling the full story of the people thrown out of work by the transition. Perhaps many drew some consolation from earlier days as seen here when smart uniforms and clean vehicles meant public service of quality.
(D.W.K.Jones)

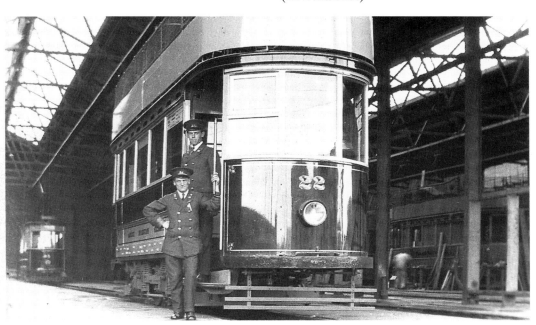